MW01009587

Workbook

For

Prepared

A Manual for Surviving Worst-Case Scenarios

(A Practical Guide to Mike Glover's Book)

Zara Press

Table of Contents

How to Use This Workbook

Welcome to the companion workbook to Mike Glover's book "Prepared: A Manual for Surviving Worst-Case Scenarios". This workbook is intended to supplement your reading experience by assisting you in applying the essential concepts and principles presented in the original book. To get the most out of this amazing workbook, follow the steps below:

Familiarize yourself with the Original Book: Before digging into this workbook, it is critical to read or comprehend the original book, "Prepared: A Manual for Surviving Worst-Case Scenarios." Remember, this workbook is meant to supplement the information in the original book, so it will make references to themes, chapters, and significant ideas from the original text.

Begin with the Summary: Start each chapter by reading the summary of corresponding chapter in the original book. This summary will give a quick review of the important ideas discussed, refreshing your memory and laying the groundwork for the reflection questions and exercises that will follow.

Examine the Key Lessons: After you've finished reading the chapter summary, go through the key lessons section. This section contains a summary of the chapter's key ideas and takeaways. Consider these teachings and how they apply to your own life and situations.

Engage in Self-Reflection: After the key lessons section, you will be presented with self-reflection questions. These questions are intended to elicit introspection and personal reflection. Take your time to think about each question and jot down your answers, thoughts and ideas in the empty spaces provided. If the spaces aren't enough, you can supplement it with a notepad or journal. Honest reflection will assist you in gaining deeper insights into your preparedness mindset and identify areas for improvement.

Complete the Implementation Exercises: Following the section dedicated to self-reflection questions, you will encounter implementation exercises. These activities are hands-on and are designed to help you apply the concepts, tips and strategies described in the original book to real-life settings. Follow the instructions provided and record your observations, plans, and actions in the space provided.

Review and Evaluate: Take a time at the conclusion of each chapter to reflect on what you have learned and done. Consider your progress, any hurdles you experienced, and methods to develop your preparedness skills even more. Doing this will improve your learning experience and allow you to get the most out of your workbook.

Final Self-Evaluation Questions: At the end of the workbook, there is a section called "Final Self-Evaluation Questions." These questions will assist you in assessing your overall progress and identifying areas where you might want to focus your ongoing learning and development efforts. Take the time to honestly answer these questions and use them as a guide for your future preparedness journey.

Take Your Time: This workbook is intended to be a companion on your journey of personal development. Allow yourself ample time and space to think thoroughly about each chapter. Avoid hurrying through the activities and instead, give yourself time to properly absorb and assimilate the information offered.

Use more materials: While this workbook gives a structured framework for contemplation, don't be afraid to look into more materials on longevity, well-being, and personal growth. Supplement your education with additional texts, podcasts, or courses that are relevant to your interests and aspirations.

Value Personalization: Keep in mind that everyone's path is unique, and the insights acquired from this workbook are unique to you. Accept the chance to personalize the exercises, change the self-reflection questions to your own situation, and tailor the workbook to your exact requirements.

Remember that this workbook is designed to supplement and expand on the information of the original book, not to replace it. You will obtain a deeper comprehension of the content and useful skills for dealing with worst-case circumstances by combining reading, contemplation, and practical tasks.

We invite you to approach this workbook with an open mind, to completely participate in the exercises, and to welcome the chance to learn and grow. May your trip through the workbook be illuminating, enlightening, and ultimately beneficial to your preparedness and resilience.

Stay alert and prepared!

Book Summary

Prepared is a well-written, comprehensive, and informative book that provides useful tips on how to prepare for any situation or eventuality. It was authored by Mike Glover, a former Special Forces Green Beret and founder of Fieldcraft Survival. The book is jam-packed with practical information on how to prepare for a variety of calamities, from natural disasters to terrorist strikes. This makes it a must-read for everyone worried about their safety and security.

Mike Glover contends in the book that most people's perceptions about preparedness are incorrect. Glover further asserts that stockpiling goods and constructing shelters will not be adequate to withstand a disaster.
True preparedness, he claims, is about developing resilient habits, skills, and abilities that will allow you to adjust and quickly adapt to any scenario.

Glover illustrates his arguments by drawing on his personal experiences as a Green Beret. He explains how he learned to survive in difficult settings and how he gained the mental fortitude to endure hardship. He also tells stories of his friends and coworkers who have overcome obstacles.

The book is structured into 3 sections: the foundation of preparedness, preparedness skills, and preparedness thinking.

"The Foundations of Preparedness," the first section, covers the significance of mindset, situational awareness, and mobility. The second section, "The Skills of Preparedness," goes through many topics including first aid, shelter construction, and fire starting. The final section, "The Mind of Preparedness," delves into the psychological aspects of surviving a disaster.

The Foundations of Preparedness

In this section of the book, Glover examines the three pillars of readiness: mindset, situational awareness, and mobility.

Mindset: According to Glover, the most significant aspect in determining whether you will survive a disaster is your mindset. He believes that you must have a positive mindset, be optimistic, be prepared to take risks, and never give up.

Situational awareness: According to Glover, you must be aware of your environment at all times. This includes being aware of where you are, who is around you, and what is going on.

Mobility: Glover believes that in an emergency, you must be able to move fast and effortlessly. This requires physical fitness as well as access to transportation.

Preparedness Skills

Glover outlines the abilities required to survive a disaster in the second section of the book. These abilities include:

First aid: According to Glover, you should be able to offer basic first aid in the event of an injury.

Shelter construction: According to Glover, knowing how to build a shelter is essential for protecting yourself from harsh weather and physical elements like rain, sunshine, snow, etc.

Fire starting: Glover claims that knowing how to build a fire is necessary for cooking food, staying warm, and signaling for assistance or help.

Water purification: According to Glover, you may not have access to clean water in the event of a catastrophe. And in order to make available to you water safe for drinking, you must first learn how to cleanse it.

Food storage: Glover believes that knowing how to keep food for lengthy periods of time is essential.

Self-defense: Glover believes that knowing how to protect yourself in the event of an assault is also important.

The Mindset of Preparedness

Glover delves into the psychological factors of surviving a disaster in the third section of the book. He claims that in the event of a disaster, you must be mentally and emotionally prepared for the hardships that await you. Among these difficulties are:

Fear: Glover claims that feeling fearful during a crisis is normal. However, you must learn to handle your fear and not allow it to immobilize you.

Loneliness: In a crisis, you may feel lonely and alone, according to Glover. You must remember, though, that you are not alone and that there are others who care about you.

Hopelessness. Glover also says that it is normal to feel hopeless when there's a crisis. However, you must have optimism and avoid giving up.

Glover closes the book by stating that being prepared is not about being afraid. It is all about being ready for anything that may come your way. He believes that developing resilient habits and abilities is the greatest approach to preparing for eventualities or crises. This involves physical fitness, the ability to think effectively under pressure, and the ability to improvise.

CHAPTER 1

The Resilient Mindset

Chapter Summary

In this chapter of the book, Glover highlights the significance of having a resilient attitude in order to survive a disaster. He maintains that the most crucial factor in determining whether you will survive a challenging scenario or difficult situation is your mindset.

A resilient mindset, according to Glover, is "the ability to bounce back from adversity and maintain a positive attitude in the face of challenges." He argues that having a resilient mindset and positive attitude is critical for surviving a disaster because it helps you to remain calm, focused, and hopeful even when circumstances are difficult.

There are several things you may do to cultivate a resilient mindset. Glover recommends the following:

Being prepared: This entails having a strategy, being aware of your resources, and being healthy and fit both physically and mentally. It also entails being knowledgeable about local dangers and understanding what to do in the case of an emergency, a crisis, or a disaster.

Possessing a positive: According to Glover, having a positive attitude does not imply that you must be happy all of the time. It simply implies that you should concentrate on the good parts of your circumstance and feel that you can overcome the difficulties you are facing.

Being adaptable: This entails being flexible and ready to think outside of the box. It also implies the ability to adjust your plans as needed.

Having a solid support system: This simply means surrounding yourself with people who care about you and on whom you can rely. These folks may provide you with emotional support, practical assistance, and a feeling of community.

Dealing with your emotions in a healthy manner: This entails finding appropriate ways to let out or express your emotions, such as talking to a therapist, writing, or exercising. It also entails avoiding harmful coping techniques such as alcohol or drug use.

Glover also emphasizes the significance of dealing with emotions in a healthy manner. In a crisis, he argues, it's acceptable to experience fear, rage, despair, and other challenging emotions. However, it is critical to find appropriate outlets for these emotions so that they do not overwhelm you.

Glover closes the chapter by stating that having a resilient attitude is not something that is innate. It's something you learn over time. The more you practice, the stronger your resilient mindset will become.

Key Lessons

Below are some of the chapter's major lessons for developing a resilient attitude.

- The most critical component in determining whether you will survive a disaster is a resilient mindset.

- You can cultivate a resilient mindset by being prepared, having a positive attitude, being adaptable, and having a solid support system.

- It's critical to remember that amid a crisis, everyone feels fear, rage, despair, and other painful emotions.

- It is critical to express these emotions in a healthy manner. The goal is to find healthy ways for expressing these emotions so that they don't overwhelm you. This can be done by:

  - Talking to a therapist, counselor, or other mental health provider.

  - Journaling about your experiences.

  - Exercising, meditating, going for a walk, or spending some time in nature.

- A resilient mindset is something you cultivate over time. The more you practice, the stronger your resilient mindset will become.

- A resilient mindset isn't about being fearful. It is about being able to face and overcome your fears.

Self-Reflection Questions

Here are some self-reflection questions to help you access your current mindset and uncover areas for improvement in developing a resilient mindset.

How prepared are you for a disaster? Do you have a strategy? Do you understand the resources available to you? Are you in good physical and mental health?

- How do you react in challenging situations? Do you prefer to concentrate on the negative or the positive? Do you feel you can overcome obstacles?

_____

_____

_____

_____

_____

_____

_____

- How do you usually react to stress and fear, and how can you enhance your capacity to manage and control these emotions in stressful situations?

_____

_____

_____

_____

_____

_____

_____

- How can you improve your mental toughness and resilience to better adapt to and overcome adversity?

_____

_____

_____

_____

_____

_____

_____

- How do you deal with uncertainty and change? What measures can you put in place to become more adaptable and embrace uncertainty with a positive mindset?

_____

_____

_____

_____

_____

_____

_____

- Are you aware of your emotional reactions in high-pressure situations? How can you properly manage your emotions in order not to lose focus and stability?

_____

_____

_____

_____

_____

_____

_____

- How do you make decisions while you're under duress? Are there any approaches or procedures you may use to ensure competent decision-making and risk assessment in difficult situations?

_____

_____

_____

_____

_____

_____

- What inspires you and keeps you hopeful in difficult times? How can you keep your feeling of purpose and optimism in order to sustain your resilience?

_____

_____

_____

_____

_____

_____

- How can you increase your mental resilience by incorporating regular training and preparation into your life? What particular workouts or drills can you do to improve your capacity to deal with worst-case scenarios?

_____

_____

_____

_____

_____

_____

_____

Implementation Exercises

By incorporating the tasks below into your routine, you may cultivate a resilient attitude that improves your ability to deal with worst-case scenarios and thrive in difficult conditions.

- *Positive Affirmations and Daily Gratitude:* Take a few minutes each day to think about three things you are grateful for. Write them down and combine them with positive affirmations that can help you stay mentally strong. To cultivate a good mentality, repeat these affirmations throughout the day.

- *Stress Management Training:* Purposefully subject yourself to controlled stressors or stimuli that resemble difficult conditions. Begin with minor stresses and progressively increase their magnitude over time. This practice helps desensitize your mind and body to stress, allowing you to deal with it more successfully in the future.

- *Simulation of Decision-Making:* Create decision-making scenarios in which you must make rapid, solid decisions under duress. Use real-life circumstances or role-playing activities to imitate them. To improve your decision-making abilities in an emergency, practice analyzing risks, considering choices, and making decisive judgments.

- *Visualization and Mental Rehearsal:* Spend time each day envisioning yourself navigating numerous worst-case circumstances effectively. Consider being cool, making sound judgments, and adjusting to difficult situations. Mental repetition or rehearsal boosts confidence and prepares your mind for different scenarios.

- ***Emotional Regulation Techniques:*** Explore several ways of regulating and managing your emotions during difficult situations. Deep breathing exercises, mindfulness meditation, and journaling can all assist you in recognizing and controlling emotional responses. To create emotional resilience, use these practices on a daily basis.

Observations, Plans, and Goals

What did you observe while completing the implementation exercises on the previous page? What are your plans and goals for the future?

_____

_____

_____

_____

_____

_____

_____

_____

_____

_____

_____

_____

_____

_____

_____

_____

_____

_____

_____

_____

_____

_____

CHAPTER 2

Planning

Chapter Summary

Glover highlights the importance of preparing and planning for a disaster in this chapter. He contends that having a plan is critical for surviving a crisis because it provides a sense of control and direction.

A plan, according to Glover, is "a roadmap for how someone will survive a crisis or catastrophe." According to him, an effective plan should include the following elements:

- An evaluation of the risks and dangers in your region.

- A list of all of your assets and resources.

- A list of your objectives and goals.

- A list of your backup plans.

The Importance of Planning

Glover opens the chapter by emphasizing the need for planning and preparing for a disaster. According to him, "The best way to prepare for the unexpected is to expect the unexpected." In a crisis, he claims that having a plan provides you with a sense of control and direction. It also assists you in being concentrated and motivated even when things are difficult.

How to Pl an for a Crisis

Glover then describes how to plan for a crisis or disaster. According to him, the first step is to identify the dangers in your location. This will assist you in identifying the precise hazards for which you must prepare. For example, if you live in a hurricane-prone location, you must ensure that you have a plan in place for evacuating your property.

The second step is to make a list of your assets and resources. This can assist you in determining what resources you have accessible in the case of a crisis. If you have a generator, for example, you will be able to keep your electricity on during a power outage.

The next stage is to write down all of your goals and objectives. This will assist you in remaining focused and motivated amid a crisis. For example, if your aim is to survive, you must ensure that you have a strategy in place for acquiring food, drink, and shelter.

The final stage is to make a list of your backup plans. This will allow you to modify your strategy if anything unexpected occurs. For example, if your original plan was to flee your house but the roads are impassable, you'll need to have a backup plan.

The Importance of Putting Your Plan into Practice

Glover closes the chapter by emphasizing the necessity of practicing your plan or putting it into action. He claims that the more you practice, the more you will be prepared for a real-world disaster. He suggests that you put your strategy into action at least once a year.

Key Lessons

Here are some key lessons from this chapter that will assist you in developing a plan for surviving a disaster. Remember that planning does not imply being paranoid. It all boils down to being ready for whatever comes your way.

- A catastrophe is an unanticipated incident that causes significant damage or loss of life. Natural catastrophes such as storms, floods, and earthquakes can trigger it, as can man-made calamities such as terrorist strikes or nuclear mishaps.

- Planning is vital for surviving any type of disaster or a catastrophe.

- It might be tough to think clearly and make sensible judgments when a disaster hits. That is why it is critical to have a plan in place before the incident occurs. This can help you maintain concentration and motivation during the crisis by giving you a sense of control and direction.

- An effective plan should include a risk assessment, a list of assets and resources, a list of goals and objectives, and a list of contingency measures.

- It is critical to put your plan into action on a regular basis once you have prepared it. This will allow you to become acquainted with the plan and ensure that it is still relevant. It will also assist you in identifying any areas that require improvement.

- It is critical to be realistic about your capabilities while developing your plan. Make no attempt to plan for everything. Instead, concentrate on the most likely dangers and how to neutralize them.

- Things don't always go as planned. That is why it is critical to be adaptable. Prepare to modify your strategy if the unexpected occurs.

- Get your family and friends involved in your plan. The more individuals who know about your plan, the better. This will assist to guarantee that everyone is on the same page and knows what to do in a crisis.

- Your plan should change in tandem with your circumstances. Make sure to update your strategy on a frequent basis to ensure that it remains current.

Self-Reflection Questions

The self-reflection questions listed below can assist you in evaluating the completeness, efficacy, and flexibility of your preparedness plan to ensure it is tailored to your individual requirements and circumstances.

Have you properly evaluated the potential risks and dangers in your situation? Are there any other hazards you should be aware of?

- In your preparedness plan, have you clearly outlined your objectives and priorities? Are they in sync with your most pressing needs in an emergency situation?

_____

_____

_____

_____

_____

_____

- Is your preparedness plan all-inclusive, addressing all facets of survival? Is there anything that needs to be developed or improved further?

_____

_____

_____

_____

_____

- How efficiently do you manage your resources? Are you monitoring and replacing your supplies on a regular basis? Are there any other means of sourcing you may try?

_____

_____

_____

_____

_____

_____

- Have you prepared well-thought-out evacuation strategies for various scenarios? Are they realistic and feasible? Do you need to practice and improve them?

_____

_____

_____

_____

_____

_____

- Have you thought about contingencies and backup plans? Are there any potential problems or eventualities in your preparedness plan that you haven't considered?

_____

_____

_____

_____

_____

_____

- Are you evaluating and revising your plan on a frequent basis? Are there any changes in your circumstances or new knowledge that may warrant alterations to your plan?

_____

_____

_____

_____

_____

_____

Implementation Exercises

You may improve your preparation for worst-case scenarios and your ability to respond successfully in difficult situations by incorporating these exercises into your routine.

- *Perform a risk assessment:* Take the time to evaluate the potential dangers and hazards in your surroundings. Determine the most likely dangers and their potential consequences. Make a list and assess its likelihood and severity. Use this information to help you plan your emergency response.

- *Create a Personal Emergency Action Plan:* Make a detailed and tailored emergency preparedness plan that addresses all areas of survival. Describe precise actions to do in various circumstances, such as shelter, food, water, medical treatment, security, and communication. The strategy should be reviewed and refined on a regular basis.

- *Practice Evacuation Drills:* Set up evacuation drills and exercises to put your preparedness plan to the test. Simulate situations in which you must escape fast and efficiently. Time yourself and note any places where you may improve. Practice evacuation procedures with family members or roommates to ensure everyone is on the same page.

- *Inventory and Rotation of Resources:* Take stock of your emergency supplies, which should include food, water, medicines, and other necessities. Create a system for tracking expiry dates and rotating perishable products on a regular basis. Make certain that your materials are well-organized, conveniently accessible, and properly stored.

- **Perform Mock Scenarios:** Create realistic fake situations to put your preparedness plan to the test. Simulate difficult scenarios and assess how effectively you respond. Examine your decision-making abilities, problem-solving abilities, and adaptability. Use these scenarios to find areas for improvement.

- **Create Communication Protocols:** Create communication methods with family, friends, and emergency contacts. In the event of an infrastructure breakdown, designate a primary and backup channel of communication. Establish frequent check-in processes and practice utilizing these communication techniques.

- **Review and Revise:** Set aside time on a regular basis to evaluate and update your preparedness plan. Keep up to date on new possible dangers or hazards. Adjust your plan as needed, taking into account changes in your surroundings, personal circumstances, and lessons learned from drills or real-life events.

Observations, Plans, and Goals

What did you observe while completing the implementation exercises on the previous page? What are your plans and goals for the future?

_____

_____

_____

_____

_____

_____

_____

_____

_____

_____

_____

_____

_____

_____

_____

_____

_____

_____

_____

_____

_____

_____

_____

CHAPTER 3

Situational Awareness

Chapter Summary

Glover highlights the importance of situational awareness in surviving a disaster in this chapter. Situational awareness, according to him, is "the ability to perceive, process, and understand the elements of your surroundings as well as the situation as a whole." He contends that situational awareness is critical for surviving a crisis because it helps you to make educated judgments and take appropriate action.

The Importance of Situational Awareness

Glover starts the chapter by emphasizing the need for situational awareness. According to him, situational awareness is "the single most important skill you can develop for surviving a catastrophe." He goes further to say that situational awareness enables you to perform the following:

- Identify potential dangers.

- Prepare for danger.

- Make sound judgments and informed decisions.

- Take the necessary actions.

How to Develop Situational Awareness

Glover then goes through methods to develop and improve situational awareness. According to him, there are three fundamental components of situational awareness:

Observation. This refers to your capacity to see and hear what is going on around you.

Interpretation. This is the ability to comprehend what you see and hear.

Decision-making. This refers to your capacity to make sound judgments based on your observations and perceptions.

Glover offers several suggestions for improving situational awareness, including:

Keep an eye on your surroundings. This entails being aware of what is going on around you, both visually and audibly.

Be mindful of your body language. This entails being conscious of your own emotional state and how it influences your perspective of the circumstance.

Be aware of your environment. This means being aware of your physical environment, such as the layout of the location, the existence of possible hazards, and the availability of supplies.

Be aware of your people. This entails being aware of the people around you, including their objectives, capabilities, and weaknesses.

Key Lessons

Here are some important takeaways from the chapter that can help you develop situational awareness and boost your chances of survival in the event of a disaster.

- The single most crucial skill you can develop to survive a disaster is situational awareness.

- Situational awareness is the capacity to observe, analyze, and comprehend the aspects of your environment as well as the overall situation. It is critical for surviving a crisis because it helps you to make informed decisions and take appropriate action.

- Situational awareness has three major components: observation, interpretation, and decision-making. The capacity to observe and hear what is going on around you is referred to as observation. The ability to understand what you see and hear is referred to as interpretation. The capacity to make informed choices based on observations and interpretations is referred to as decision-making.

- Situational awareness is more than just being aware of possible hazards. It is also important to be aware of opportunities. You'll be more likely to spot possibilities to escape, obtain aid, or take other measures that will increase your chances of survival if you're aware of your surroundings.

- You must be aware of your surroundings, body language, environment, and people in order to develop situational awareness.

You must also be attentive to details, curious, open-minded, and proactive.

- Situational awareness is not something that is innate. It's something you learn over time. The more you practice, the better you'll get.

- Situational awareness may be developed in a variety of ways. You may attend classes, study books, or simply practice being aware of your environment.

Self-Reflection Questions

These self-reflection questions will assist you in evaluating the efficacy of your observation, evaluation, adaption, and decision-making skills, as well as identifying areas for improvement.

- How well do you observe and collect information from your surroundings? Is there any area of your life where you often overlook key details or fail to see possible threats?

_____

_____

_____

_____

_____

_____

- How effectively do you assess possible hazards and risks in various situations? Do you actively look for indicators of danger and evaluate suspicious behavior? Are there any biases or blind spots that might impair your ability to assess risks accurately?

_____

_____

_____

_____

_____

_____

_____

- How well do you understand human behavior and how it affects your safety? Are you able to analyze body language and environmental indicators to determine a person's intents and possible threats? Are there any areas of human behavior that you need to research more or improve?

_____

_____

_____

_____

_____

_____

_____

- How well do you manage distractions and focus in high-stress situations? Do you have plans in place to filter out extraneous information while remaining alert? Is there anything that frequently interferes with your situational awareness?

_____

_____

_____

_____

_____

_____

_____

- How well do you adapt to changing conditions and modify your situational awareness? Are you flexible in your assessment and decision-making? Do you actively seek out fresh information and make adjustments to your plans and responses as needed?

  _____

  _____

  _____

  _____

  _____

  _____

  _____

- Can you make sound judgments based on your situational awareness? Do you assimilate information fast and weigh diverse options? How certain are you of your ability to prioritize actions depending on perceived danger level and available resources?

  _____

  _____

  _____

  _____

  _____

  _____

  _____

- How dedicated are you to constantly enhancing your situational awareness? Do you regularly train, practice, or seek feedback to improve your observation, evaluation, and decision-making abilities? Is there anything, in particular, you'd like to work on to improve?

_____

_____

_____

_____

_____

_____

_____

Implementation Exercises

The tasks in this section are designed to help you develop and improve your situational awareness skills in tangible and practical ways. You may create a heightened sense of awareness, increase threat assessment abilities, and make better-informed decisions in a variety of circumstances by engaging in the exercises.

- *Daily Observation Practice:* **Set** some time each day to work on your observation abilities and skills. Select a location or circumstance and pay close attention to details and indications in your surroundings. Make an effort to notice details that you may have missed earlier.

- *Threat Assessment Scenarios:* Make scenarios or simulations to evaluate potential hazards and dangers. Utilize a variety of venues or scenarios, such as congested areas or new sites. To improve your threat assessment skills, practice spotting suspicious actions and assessing potential threats.

- *Human Behavior Study:* Select a specific component of human behavior to study in-depth, such as body language or vocal cues. To deepen your understanding and broaden your knowledge, read books, and articles, or enroll in online courses. Apply your knowledge by studying individuals in diverse circumstances to identify patterns and signs.

- *Minimizing Distraction Challenge:* Set up a day or a certain time period to intentionally reduce distractions in your area. Remove technological gadgets, reduce background noise, and create a concentrated setting to improve your ability to maintain situational awareness.

- *Adaptive Scenario Training:* Set up adaptive scenario training sessions in which you purposely include unexpected elements or changes. Practice adapting your situational awareness to changing conditions and making rapid decisions based on fresh information.

- *Decision-Making Exercises:* Create decision-making drills that test your ability to make rapid informed decisions with little information. Create time-limited situations and practice analyzing alternatives, assessing risks, and choosing the best course of action.

- *Real-Life Observation Journal:* Keep a diary to record your observations from your daily life. Details about your environment, people's behavior, and any possible hazards or risks you see should be documented. Examine your journal on a regular basis to spot patterns, areas for improvement, and any gaps in your situational awareness.

Observations, Plans, and Goals

What did you observe while completing the implementation exercises on the previous page? What are your plans and goals for the future?

_____

_____

_____

_____

_____

_____

_____

_____

_____

_____

_____

_____

_____

_____

_____

_____

_____

_____

_____

_____

_____

_____

_____

CHAPTER 4

Decision Point

Chapter Summary

Glover highlights the necessity of making excellent decisions amid a crisis in this chapter. He contends that being able to make fast informed judgments is critical for survival.

The Importance of Decision-Making

Glover opens the chapter by emphasizing the importance of making decisions in a crisis. According to him, "the ability to make quick and informed decisions is essential for survival." He also says that "the difference between life and death in a crisis often comes down to the choices you make."

He then discusses the types of decisions that you may need to make in a crisis. According to him, these decisions might vary from little, everyday decisions to major, life-or-death ones. For example, you may have to choose whether to run or stay in your house, whether to fight or flee, or whether to trust someone you don't know.

Factors That Influence Decision-Making

Glover then goes over the variables that might impact your decision-making in a crisis. These aspects, according to him, include your training, experience, emotions, and surroundings.

Training: In a crisis, your training might assist you make better decisions. You will be better familiar with the sorts of decisions that you may need to make and the factors that you must examine if you have been trained in crisis management or emergency response.

Experience: In a crisis, your experience might also assist you make better judgments. If you have already experienced a crisis, you will have a better knowledge of what to expect and how to react.

Emotions: In a crisis, your emotions might also impact your decision-making. It might be difficult to think properly and make sound decisions when you are terrified or angry.

Environment: In a crisis, your surroundings or environment might also have an impact on your decision-making. It might be tough to make the right decisions when you are in a risky or unfamiliar setting.

Making Sound Decisions in a Crisis

Glover went on to offer a variety of suggestions for making sound decisions in a crisis. He recommends that you:

Be aware of your surroundings. The more you learn about your surroundings, the better decisions you will be able to make.

Consider your alternatives. Before making a decision, weigh all of the possibilities and options available to you.

Be decisive. Always be quick to make decisions.

Be flexible. Be ready to adjust your viewpoint or change your mind if circumstances change.

Be confident in yourself. Have faith in your capacity to make sound decisions.

Glover closes the chapter by stating that making good decisions in a crisis isn't something one is born with. Instead, it is a skill that can be learned and improved. He advises readers to practice making decisions in a variety of scenarios so that they will be ready if a crisis occurs.

Key Lessons

In a crisis, being able to make quick informed decisions is critical for survival. If you can't make good decisions under duress, your chances of survival are slim.

- In a crisis, the types of decisions that you may need to make might range from simple, everyday decisions to huge, life-or-death ones.

- Your training, experience, emotions, and environment may all have an impact on your decision-making in a crisis.

- When making judgments in a crisis, you should be aware of your surroundings, be aware of your alternatives, and be decisive, flexible, and confident.

  - *Being aware of your surroundings:* You will be better able to assess the situation and make informed decisions if you are aware of your surroundings. For example, if you are trapped in a burning building, you must be aware of the exits and any threats in order to escape safely.

  - *Being aware of your options:* When making a decision, it is critical to be aware of all of your options. This will assist you in making the best choice for the scenario. For example, if you become lost in the woods, you must be aware of all of your alternatives for returning to civilization.

  - *Being decisive:* It is critical to make quick decisions in a crisis. If you wait too long to make a decision, you may miss out on a chance. If you are assaulted, for example, you must make a rapid decision on whether to fight or run.

- **_Being adaptable:_** Things don't always go as planned in a crisis. It is critical to be adaptable and open to adjusting your plans if required. For instance, if you are traveling and meet traffic congestion, you must be flexible and locate another route.

- **_Being confident:_** In a crisis, it is critical to have faith in your ability to make good decisions. You will be more likely to make the right decisions and survive the crisis if you are confident. For example, if you are making a presentation and begin to feel worried, you must remain confident in your abilities to give the presentation.

- There is no one-size-fits-all solution to making decisions in a crisis. The best options will differ based on the circumstances.

- Practice is the best technique to enhance your decision-making abilities. The more you practice, the better you'll get at making rapid and educated decisions under duress.

- It's critical to realize that you're not alone. In a crisis, there are those who can assist you in making sound decisions. If you are having difficulty, ask people for help.

Self-Reflection Questions

The following self-reflection questions are intended to foster introspection and self-evaluation of your decision-making abilities. You may find areas for improvement in your decision-making processes during difficult situations by reflecting on and answering these questions.

- How effectively do you evaluate the circumstances before making important decisions? Are you meticulous when gathering information and assessing risks, or do you make quick decisions without a clear comprehension of the situation?

_____

_____

_____

_____

_____

_____

- How good are you at prioritizing your actions at decision points? Do you know what tasks are most urgent and necessary, or do you struggle to establish the best sequence in which to do them?

_____

_____

_____

_____

_____

_____

_____

- How good are you at weighing the risks and advantages of various options? Do you thoroughly analyze the possible outcomes and repercussions, or do you make decisions without completely assessing the risks and rewards?

_____

_____

_____

_____

_____

_____

_____

- How well do you keep your cool in high-pressure situations? Do you have the ability to control stress and keep emotions from clouding your judgment, or do you frequently make decisions based on fear or anxiety?

_____

_____

_____

_____

_____

_____

_____

- What kind of contingency measures do you have in place for unforeseen events? Do you have backup plans and other lines of action in place, or do you get overwhelmed or trapped when confronted with unexpected challenges?

_____

_____

_____

_____

_____

_____

- How successfully do you use the resources at your disposal during decision points? Do you have the ability to appraise your skills, knowledge, and physical assets in order to make educated decisions, or do you struggle to identify and exploit your available resources?

_____

_____

_____

_____

_____

_____

_____

- How serious are you about learning from your previous decision-making experiences? Do you engage in self-reflection and debriefing after important moments to find areas for improvement, or do you simply go on without analyzing and learning from your decisions?

_____

_____

_____

_____

_____

_____

_____

Implementation Exercises

These implementation exercises are designed to help you build and improve your decision-making abilities in practical and immersive ways.

By actively engaging in these exercises, you may increase your ability to assess situations, prioritize tasks, evaluate risks, handle stress, and make informed choices during important decision points.

For maximum impact, remember to apply the lessons acquired from these exercises to real-life situations.

- *Scenario Role-playing:* Try creating decision-making scenarios based on various worst-case scenarios. Role-play such scenarios with a spouse, partner, friend, or group, taking turns to make important decisions and analyzing the results. Discuss and evaluate the efficacy of each decision taken.

- *Decision Journal:* Start a decision journal in which you document crucial decisions you make in your everyday life. Consider the steps that led up to each decision, the options examined, and the results. Review the journal on a regular basis to uncover patterns, areas for improvement, and the lessons learned.

- *Time-Pressured Decision-Making:* Schedule time-limited decision-making activities. Make a list of chores or challenges and set a time limit for yourself to make decisions and take action. Practice thinking on your feet, prioritizing tasks, and making quick decisions.

- ***Case Study Analysis:*** Look at real-life survival tales or historical events when people had to make difficult decisions. Analyze the people's actions, the repercussions, and the lessons learned. Discuss and consider how you would handle similar circumstances.

- ***Simulation Training:*** Participate in simulation training activities that simulate difficult events, such as virtual reality programs, escape rooms, or outdoor survival courses, to practice decision-making under realistic, high-pressure settings. Examine the results of your decisions and find out areas for improvement.

- ***Decision-Making Review Board:*** Create a decision-making review board comprised of trusted persons who can offer impartial feedback on your decision-making abilities. Present them with circumstances or decisions you made and solicit their feedback. Use these suggestions to improve your decision-making process.

- ***Take Deliberate Risks:*** Participate in purposeful risk-taking activities in safe and regulated situations. This might be anything from adventure sports to outdoor activities to public speaking. Push your limits, learn risk assessment, and make rational decisions while controlling your fear and adrenaline.

Observations, Plans, and Goals

What did you observe while completing the implementation exercises on the previous page? What are your plans and goals for the future?

_____

_____

_____

_____

_____

_____

_____

_____

_____

_____

_____

_____

_____

_____

_____

_____

_____

_____

_____

_____

_____

_____

_____

CHAPTER 5

Everyday Carry (EDC)

Chapter Summary

Glover explains the benefits of having an Everyday Carry (EDC) gear in this chapter. He claims that having an EDC kit is beneficial for a variety of reasons.

To begin, an EDC kit can assist you in being prepared for unforeseen events. If there's a sudden storm, having a flashlight and a raincoat will come in handy. Second, an EDC kit can assist you in staying safe. If you're coming home late at night, for example, having a knife or multi-tool for self-defense will come in handy. Finally, an EDC kit can assist you in surviving a big crisis. If there is a power outage or a natural disaster, having a flashlight, a first-aid kit, and other essential items will come in handy.

Glover starts by explaining what an EDC kit is. An EDC kit, according to him, is a tiny, portable collection of essential items that you may keep with you at all times. Your EDC kit should include items that you might need in a range of scenarios, such as a flashlight, multi-tool, first-aid kit, and knife.

Glover then goes over the many sorts of EDC kits that may be assembled. He claims that there is no such thing as a one-size-fits-all EDC kit, and that the contents in your kit will vary based on your own requirements and circumstances. He does, however, give some fundamental suggestions for assembling an EDC kit.

- Your EDC kit should contain items that you would genuinely use. Don't just assemble a kit of random items that you believe you might need someday. Make a kit out of stuff that you would use in a real-world circumstance.

- Your EDC kit should contain items that are small and light. You don't want to be carrying a large backpack full of items around all day. Your emergency preparedness package should be compact enough to fit in your pocket or handbag.

- Your EDC kit should contain high-quality items. You don't want to assemble a kit out of inexpensive, disposable items. The things in your EDC kit should be long-lasting and dependable.

Glover then makes some specific suggestions for items to add to your EDC kit. He recommends having a flashlight, multi-tool, first-aid kit, knife, fire starter, water bottle, and survival guide.

Glover closes the chapter by reminding readers of the need for an EDC kit in order to be prepared for the unexpected. He advises readers to assemble an EDC kit and have it with them at all times.

Key Lessons

- An EDC kit is an important tool for staying safe and prepared. Carrying a few important items with you at all times allows you to be more prepared to deal with a range of unforeseen scenarios.

- Your EDC kit should be personalized to your specific requirements and situations. There is no such thing as a one-size-fits-all EDC kit, so think about which items might be most beneficial to you.

- Determine the precise hazards and scenarios that you are likely to face in your environment. Consider temperature, location, and personal activities to determine the basic items that would be most beneficial to have on hand.

- It is critical to keep your EDC kit up to date. Your kit's contents may need to be adjusted as your requirements and circumstances change.

- You should constantly practice utilizing the items in your EDC kit. This will help you become acquainted with them so you can apply them efficiently in an emergency.

- Your EDC kit should contain items that are small, light, high quality, and durable. Also, make sure that the items in it are things that you would genuinely use and not just random items that you believe you might need someday.

Self-Reflection Questions

The self-reflection questions below are intended to assist you in evaluating the alignment of your EDC with your specific needs, the functionality and dependability of your gear, your ability to strike a balance between portability and capability, the frequency with which you reassess your gear, your proficiency in using your EDC items, and your compliance with relevant laws and regulations.

By answering these questions honestly, you may discover areas for improvement and ensure that your Everyday Carry is suited to your preparedness needs.

- Have you evaluated your individual needs and probable threats in your location to choose which items to put in your Everyday Carry? How well prepared are you for any crises or worst-case scenarios that may arise?

_____

_____

_____

_____

_____

_____

_____

- Are you putting utility first in your EDC selection? Do your chosen items have many applications and provide versatile solutions to a variety of possible situations?

_____

_____

_____

_____

_____

_____

_____

- How happy are you with the quality and dependability of the gadgets in your Everyday Carry? Have you made investments in well-known brands and goods that are recognized for their longevity and performance?

_____

_____

_____

_____

_____

_____

_____

- Is there a balance between the mobility and capability of your EDC? Are your EDC items small and light enough for you to carry comfortably every day while also giving you the capability needed to deal with potential emergencies?

_____

_____

_____

_____

_____

_____

_____

- How frequently do you review and update your EDC? Do you frequently examine your EDC items to ensure it stays relevant and effective in light of changes in your environment, personal circumstances, and technological advancements?

_____

_____

_____

_____

_____

_____

_____

- How knowledgeable are you about the items in your Everyday Carry? Have you sought training and practiced on a regular basis to get the knowledge and abilities required to efficiently use them?

_____

_____

_____

_____

_____

_____

_____

- Are you aware of, and in compliance with, the rules and regulations governing the ownership and transportation of specific items in your Everyday Carry? Do you keep up to date on any legal limits or regulations that may relate to the items you carry?

_____

_____

_____

_____

_____

_____

_____

Implementation Exercises

The exercises provided in this section are intended to help you improve your Everyday Carry (EDC) and build the skills needed to use your gear effectively in real-life circumstances.

While carrying out these exercises, remember to prioritize safety, acquire adequate training, and follow any applicable rules or regulations.

- *EDC Audit and Optimization:* Perform a comprehensive review of your existing Everyday Carry items. Examine the functionality, relevance, and dependability of each item. Identify any gaps or areas for improvement in your EDC and optimize them by replacing or upgrading things as needed.

- *EDC Scenario Challenges:* Create a set of simulated scenarios that illustrate possible worst-case scenarios. Use your EDC items to navigate and conquer these obstacles, putting the item's use and efficacy to the test in real-world circumstances.

- *EDC Skill Development:* Identify the skills that can help you use your EDC items more efficiently. Make time to practice, train, or seek advice from professionals in relevant industries to develop and improve these skills.

- *EDC Maintenance and Readiness:* Create a regimen for maintaining your EDC items to guarantee they are always in good working order. Make a checklist to examine, clean, and replace batteries or components on a regular basis to keep your items in working order.

- ***EDC Innovation and Research:*** Stay up to date on the latest advances in EDC technology, gear, and techniques. Research and test novel ideas that might improve the usefulness, mobility, and efficacy of your Everyday Carry.

- ***EDC Integration into Everyday Life:*** Evaluate how effectively your EDC integrates into your everyday routine. Experiment with various methods of carrying and accessing your EDC items for the best ease and comfort. Optimize your EDC configuration to suit your lifestyle.

- ***Partnerships for EDC Training:*** Collaborate with like-minded folks or join a group focused on preparedness and EDC. Share information, discuss experiences, and take part in collaborative training activities to improve your understanding and skills with your EDC items.

Observations, Plans, and Goals

What did you observe while completing the implementation exercises on the previous page? What are your plans and goals for the future?

_____

_____

_____

_____

_____

_____

_____

_____

_____

_____

_____

_____

_____

_____

_____

_____

_____

_____

_____

_____

_____

_____

_____

CHAPTER 6

Mobility

Chapter Summary

Glover explores the need for mobility in a survival situation in this chapter. He contends that the ability to move fast and effectively can be the difference between escaping danger and losing your life when there is a crisis.

Glover goes further to talk about the various things that might affect your mobility in an emergency. He then goes over some of the things you can do to improve your mobility, such as staying fit and in shape, knowing how to use multiple forms of transportation, and having the right gear.

The Importance of Mobility

Glover contends that one of the most vital survival skills is mobility. According to him, "Being able to move quickly and efficiently can mean the difference between life and death." This is due to the fact that mobility allows you to:

- *Get to safety:* If you find yourself in a dangerous situation, mobility can help you get to safety. If you are caught in a fire, for example, you can flee to a safe spot.

- *Find food and water:* If you're stranded or lost, mobility can aid you in finding food and water. For example, if you are hiking in the bush, you can stop and get food and drink.

- *Evade predators:* If you are being pursued by a predator, your mobility will help you escape. If you are being pursued by a bear, for example, you can flee to a safe spot.

Factors Influencing Mobility

A variety of things might impact your mobility in a survival situation. These factors are as follows:

- *Your physical condition:* The better your fitness level, the easier it will be to move quickly and efficiently.

- *The landscape you are traversing:* Certain terrain is more difficult to navigate than others. Moving through dense woodland, for example, is more difficult than moving through open fields.

- *The weather conditions:* The weather might also have an impact on your mobility. Moving, for example, becomes more difficult under heavy rain or snow.

How to Improve Your Mobility

- In a survival situation, there are several things you may do to improve your mobility. These are some examples:

- ***Staying in shape:*** This is one of the best strategies to increase your mobility. This includes frequent exercise and a nutritious diet.

- ***Learning to use various kinds of transportation:*** This will provide you with more options and additional alternatives during a crisis or in a survival situation. If you know how to ride a bicycle, for example, you may utilize it to go long distances.

- ***Having the proper gear:*** Things like a backpack, first aid kit, map, and compass can help you stay mobile in a survival emergency.

Mobility Strategies

In a survival situation, you might employ a variety of mobility strategies. Among these strategies are:

Planning your route: Before you take off, spend some time planning your route. This will assist you in avoiding obstacles and traveling efficiently.

Using several modes of transportation: If feasible, travel by using multiple modes of transportation. If one form of transportation becomes unavailable, you will have other options.

Being aware of your surroundings: Keep an eye out for any threats and pay attention to your surroundings. This will assist you in avoiding accidents and being safe.

Glover closes the chapter by restating the importance of mobility in survival. He advises readers to improve their movement and be prepared to move quickly and efficiently during a crisis.

Key Lessons

Mobility is very important for survival. Being able to move fast and effectively might be the difference between life and death in a survival situation.

- A variety of factors might have an impact on your mobility. These variables include your physical fitness, the terrain you are traversing, and the weather conditions.

- There are things you can do to improve your mobility. Some of them involve staying in shape, understanding how to use various forms of transportation, and carrying the proper gear.

- Planning your route is critical. Take some time to organize your trip before you go. This will assist you in avoiding obstacles and going in the most effective manner possible.

- It is a good idea to use several forms of transportation. If one form of transportation becomes unavailable, you will have other possibilities.

- Keep an eye out for any threats and pay attention to your surroundings. This will assist you in avoiding accidents and being safe.

Self-Reflection Questions

The questions below are meant to help you assess your physical fitness, navigation abilities, adaptability, gear, load management, situational awareness, and overall readiness for effective mobility.

By reflecting on these questions, you may find areas for improvement and take action to enhance your mobility.

- Have you evaluated your present level of fitness and mobility? How prepared are you for challenging situations that may necessitate lengthy durations of physical exertion and movement?

_____

_____

_____

_____

_____

_____

_____

- How good are your navigating skills? Can you read maps, use a compass, and navigate new territory successfully without relying much on technology?

_____

_____

_____

_____

_____

_____

_____

- Do you have a good awareness of the unique mobility problems you could experience in your area or at the places you frequent? Have you made efforts to gain the required skills and knowledge to effectively navigate these challenges?

_____

_____

_____

_____

_____

_____

_____

- Have you evaluated your mobility gear and equipment? Are your bag, boots, and other essentials appropriate for the conditions you may face? Are they lightweight, robust, and appropriate for your mobility requirements?

_____

_____

_____

_____

_____

_____

_____

- How adaptive are you in terms of changing your mobility strategies? Can you swiftly change your plans in response to changing conditions or unexpected obstacles? How willing are you to try new movement techniques and adapt to varied terrains?

  _____

  _____

  _____

  _____

  _____

  _____

- Are you aware of the significance of load management in maintaining mobility? Have you examined the contents of your backpack or go-bag to verify that they are necessary and correctly distributed to minimize undue effort and fatigue?

  _____

  _____

  _____

  _____

  _____

  _____

- What level of situational awareness do you have? Do you actively monitor and analyze your environment to detect any risks or challenges to your mobility? How can you increase your ability to remain aware and make sound judgments while moving?

_____

_____

_____

_____

_____

_____

_____

Implementation Exercises

The exercises below are intended to help you improve your mobility, physical fitness, and adaptability in diverse settings.

By actively engaging in the exercises, you can acquire practical skills, improve your navigation abilities, optimize your load management, and prepare for mobility issues in worst-case circumstances

While carrying out these exercises, remember to prioritize safety, seek adequate training, and follow any applicable rules or regulations.

- *Map Reading and Navigation Challenge:* Pick an unknown region or path and practice your map reading and navigation abilities. Plan your route with a topographic map, set waypoints, and navigate the terrain with a compass. Take note of landmarks and natural features to improve your navigating skills.

- *Fitness and Mobility Training:* Create an all-encompassing fitness and mobility training plan. Include activities that will help you increase your endurance, strength, flexibility, and balance. Hiking, sprinting, climbing, and functional motions may all be used to imitate real-life mobility conditions.

- *Load Management Evaluation:* Examine the weight and contents of your present go-bag or backpack. Determine which things may be reduced or replaced with lighter alternatives. Practice packing and adjusting your load to help you maximize weight distribution and decrease strain when moving.

- *Terrain Familiarization:* Choose several terrain types that are found in your geographical location or probable survival scenarios. Spend some time exploring and becoming acquainted with these terrains, as well as practicing efficient movement tactics and detecting any impediments or hurdles.

- *Practicing Waterborne Mobility:* If water mobility is a factor, look for chances to practice water skills. To improve your mobility capabilities in water, learn basic swimming techniques, learn how to paddle a kayak or canoe, or take a boating safety course.

- *Adaptability circumstances:* Create simulated circumstances in which you must modify your mobility methods. Set problems that require you to rethink your plans, take a different route, or face unanticipated barriers. To improve your adaptability, practice thinking on your feet and establishing flexible reactions.

- *Team Mobility Exercises:* Participate in mobility exercises with a group of like-minded people. Group walks, orienteering activities, and wilderness navigation challenges should be planned and carried out. To improve collective mobility skills, collaborate, share knowledge, and learn from one another's experiences.

Observations, Plans, and Goals

What did you observe while completing the implementation exercises on the previous page? What are your plans and goals for the future?

_____

_____

_____

_____

_____

_____

_____

_____

_____

_____

_____

_____

_____

_____

_____

_____

_____

_____

_____

_____

_____

_____

CHAPTER 7

Homestead

Chapter Summary

Glover explains the value of having a homestead in a survival situation in this chapter. He starts by explaining the importance of a homestead.

Then he goes further to talk about the many considerations to consider while selecting a homestead location. These characteristics include water availability, soil quality, closeness to resources, and the likelihood of natural disasters. He then goes over some of the steps you could take to prepare your home for a survival situation. These include things like constructing a shelter, growing a garden, and stockpiling food and water.

The Importance of a Homestead

Glover believes that establishing a homestead is one of the most effective strategies to prepare for a survival emergency. According to him, "A homestead can provide you with a safe place to live, food to eat, and water to drink." This is due to the fact that a homestead allows you to:

Be self-sufficient: You can cultivate your own food, raise your own animals, and gather your own water if you have a homestead. This means that in a survival emergency, you will not be reliant on outside resources.

Be safe: In a survival situation, a homestead may offer you a safe location to dwell. You may construct a shelter to protect yourself from natural elements and establish a garden to produce food.

Be comfortable: In a survival situation, a homestead may give you a comfortable location to live. You may design a house that meets your requirements and grow a garden that feeds you with fresh food.

Choosing a Homestead site

When selecting a homestead location, there are several variables to consider. These elements are as follows:

Water availability: You will need a consistent source of water for drinking, cooking, and bathing.

Soil quality: You'll need soil that's suitable for producing crops.

The accessibility of resources: You'll need to be near supplies like firewood, building materials, and tools.

Natural disaster risk: You must select a location that is not vulnerable to natural catastrophes such as floods, earthquakes, or wildfires.

Planning Your Homestead

After deciding on a homestead site, you must prepare it for a survival situation. The steps to take to do this are:

Building a shelter: To protect yourself from the elements, you will need to construct a shelter.

Planting a garden: In order to supply food for yourself, you will need to grow a garden.

Food and water storage: You will need to store food and water in case of an emergency.

Learning survival skills: Survival skills such as hunting, fishing, and first aid will be required.

Glover closes the chapter by emphasizing the importance of a homestead in a survival situation. He advises readers to begin planning their homestead as soon as possible.

Key Lessons

- A homestead may offer you with a secure place to live, food, and water. This is due to the fact that a homestead allows you to:

  - Cultivate your own food, raise your own animals, and collect your own water. This means that in a survival situation, you will not be reliant on outside resources.

  - Have a safe location to dwell. That's because construct a shelter to protect yourself from the elements.

  - Have a comfortable place to live in during a crisis. This is due to the fact that you can design a house that meets your needs in a homestead.

- When selecting a homestead site, take into account the availability of water, the quality of the soil, the accessibility to resources, and the risk of natural catastrophes. These characteristics will have an impact on your ability to stay on your homestead, therefore it is critical to select a location that is well-suited to your needs.

- After deciding on a homestead location, you must prepare it for a survival crisis by constructing a shelter, establishing a garden, and stockpiling food and water. These are critical stages in ensuring you have the resources you need to live if the outside world is disturbed.

- It is recommended that you learn survival skills such as hunting, fishing, and first aid. These abilities will help you survive in a variety of situations, and they will be especially useful if you live on a homestead.

- A homestead will give you a chance to reconnect with nature while also living a more sustainable lifestyle. A homestead might be a terrific alternative for you if you want to live a more self-sufficient and ecologically responsible lifestyle.

- There are several methods for establishing a homestead. The ideal method for you will be determined by your unique circumstances and demands. However, there are several tools available to assist you in getting started, so don't be afraid to do your homework and find what works for you.

- It is critical to begin preparing your homestead as soon as possible. This will give you enough time to choose the ideal site, construct your shelter, and plant your garden. It will also allow you to learn vital survival skills and prepare for any possible challenges.

Self-Reflection Questions

Here are some self-reflection questions to stimulate introspection and self-assessment about your readiness to construct a homestead in the event of a catastrophe.

The questions will assist you in assessing your level of self-sufficiency, geographic compatibility, sustainable practices, security measures, skill development, and community involvement.

You may discover areas for improvement and take meaningful measures toward a more resilient homesteading lifestyle by reflecting on these questions.

- Have you assessed your present level of self-sufficiency? How prepared are you to meet your basic requirements on your own, taking into account things such as food production, energy generation, and water supply?

_____

_____

_____

_____

_____

_____

_____

- Have you considered if your current site is suitable for building a homestead? Does it have the resources, climatic conditions, and security measures needed for a sustainable and resilient homestead?

_____

_____

_____

_____

_____

_____

- What actions have you taken to create long-term food production systems? How knowledgeable are you about gardening, livestock management, and alternative agricultural methods? How can you hone your skills in these areas?

_____

_____

_____

_____

_____

_____

- Have you given any thought to living off the grid? How well do you understand renewable energy sources, rainwater harvesting, and waste management systems? What steps can you take to improve your self-reliance in these areas?

_____

_____

_____

_____

_____

_____

- How have you tackled the subject of home security and defence? Have you identified possible risks and put suitable measures in place? What more precautions can you take to protect your property and loved ones?

_____

_____

_____

_____

_____

_____

_____

- What practical skills have you learned to help you live a homesteading lifestyle? Do you have the requisite skills and expertise in areas like building, food preservation, and first aid? How can you continue to hone these skills?

_____

_____

_____

_____

_____

_____

- Have you made contacts with like-minded people or a homesteading community? How can you participate actively in information sharing, cooperation, and mutual assistance to improve your readiness and resilience?

_____

_____

_____

_____

_____

_____

Implementation Exercises

Here are some implementation exercises to help you take practical steps toward establishing a resilient homestead.

- *Perform a Self-Sufficiency Audit:* Determine your present degree of self-sufficiency and areas for improvement. Set clear targets for food production, energy generation, and water supply, and devise a strategy to improve your self-sufficiency in each.

- *Investigate and Select a Suitable Homestead Location:* Conduct extensive research on prospective homestead locations depending on your requirements and interests. Consider factors such as water availability, fertile soil, climatic conditions, closeness to resources, and security. Choose the best place for your new homestead based on these factors.

- *Sustainable Food Production project:* Start a project for sustainable food production, such as planting a vegetable garden, keeping backyard hens, or exploring hydroponics. Begin small and progressively increase your production capacity to meet a large portion of your food demands.

- *Implement Off-Grid Solutions:* Take practical actions to increase your energy and water self-sufficiency. To create power, install solar panels or other renewable energy technologies. Explore rainwater gathering and purification technologies to secure your water supply.

- *Improve Security Measures:* Evaluate your home's security and find areas that need to be improved. Install strong fences, security cameras, or motion-activated lighting. To guarantee your safety, create an emergency communication plan and conduct drills.

- *Learn and Put Essential Homesteading Skills to Use:* Identify critical homesteading skills such as carpentry, food preservation, first aid, and permaculture. Enrol in related classes, seminars, or online tutorials to learn and practice these skills.

- *Connect with the Homesteading Community:* Look for local homesteading clubs, workshops, or online forums to meet like-minded people. Participate in meetings or activities where you may share information, and resources, and establish a supportive network of fellow homesteaders.

Observations, Plans, and Goals

What did you observe while completing the implementation exercises on the previous page? What are your plans and goals for the future?

_____

_____

_____

_____

_____

_____

_____

_____

_____

_____

_____

_____

_____

_____

_____

_____

_____

_____

_____

_____

_____

Final Self-Assessment Questions

- Did you meet the objectives you set for yourself at the start of this workbook? If not, what were the impediments to your progress?

_____

_____

_____

_____

_____

_____

- Reflecting on your journey through this workbook, what are your greatest accomplishments? What are your thoughts on your overall progress?

_____

_____

_____

_____

_____

_____

- How has your self-awareness evolved as you worked through this workbook? Have you got new insights on your preparedness strengths, shortcomings, attitudes, or beliefs?

_____

_____

_____

_____

_____

_____

- What particular improvements in yourself or changes in belief have you experienced as a result of working through the exercises and activities in this workbook?

_____

_____

_____

_____

_____

_____

- Which abilities did you improve or learn as a result of this workbook? How confident are you in those areas right now, compared to when you first started?

_____

_____

_____

_____

_____

_____

_____

- Are there any skills or knowledge gaps that you have discovered as a result of this workbook? If so, what measures are you planning to take to address them?

_____

_____

_____

_____

_____

_____

_____

- How well did you apply the principles, tactics, and approaches you learned in this workbook to real-life circumstances or challenges?

_____

_____

_____

_____

_____

_____

_____

- Can you give instances of how you've used the workbook content in your everyday life?

_____

_____

_____

_____

_____

_____

_____

- What were the most significant barriers or problems you faced while working through this workbook? How did you get past them?

_____

_____

_____

_____

_____

_____

_____

- How have you developed or boosted your resilience as a result of confronting and overcoming these challenges?

_____

_____

_____

_____

_____

_____

_____

- Reflecting on your wellbeing before and after completing this workbook, what positive changes in your physical, mental, or emotional health have you observed?

  _____

  _____

  _____

  _____

  _____

  _____

- What are the primary areas you want to continue working on or improve in the future, based on your self-assessment and reflections?

  _____

  _____

  _____

  _____

  _____

  _____

- What concrete actions will you take to preserve and improve on the progress you've achieved with this workbook?

  _____

  _____

  _____

  _____

  _____

  _____

  _____

- How has the process of engaging with this workbook content influenced your overall perspective, abilities, and preparedness?

  _____

  _____

  _____

  _____

  _____

  _____

  _____

- What are your future objectives and areas of concentration for improving your preparedness as a result of the knowledge and insights obtained from this workbook?

  _____

  _____

  _____

  _____

  _____

  _____

  _____

Made in United States
Troutdale, OR
04/05/2024

18958975R00055